REUSABLE CALENDAR

THE HIDDEN CURRICULUM

ONE-A-DAY CALENDAR

NOTE:
Please read the whole calendar upright (using the front of each page), then flip the book for the rest of the year. Don't worry, we will tell you when to flip your calendar!

The Hidden Curriculum
One-A-Day Calendar

All marketing and publishing rights guaranteed to and reserved by:

FUTURE HORIZONS

(817) 277-0727
www.fhautism.com

© 2024 Brenda Smith Myles
All rights reserved.

No part of this product may be reproduced in any manner whatsoever without written permission of Future Horizons, Inc., except in the case of brief quotations embodied in reviews or unless noted within the book.

ISBN: 9781957984995

— *Introduction* —

This unique calendar has been created to make the learning of hidden curriculum items a natural and painless part of everyday life, just like brushing your teeth or turning the pages of a calendar.

The Hidden Curriculum refers to those unstated rules, assumptions, expectations, or customs that, if not understood, can make the world a confusing place and make us feel isolated and out of it. Most of us like rules if they are consistent. It is when they are unclear, are used inconsistently, or are unstated that we become upset, indignant, or confused.

Some learn the hidden curriculum almost automatically. Others learn it only by direct instruction and practice. And that's where this calendar comes in. It contains a variety of hidden curriculum items that are difficult for many to understand without direct instruction.

Hidden curriculum items in this calendar can be used across ages and grades (K through 12). Because hidden curriculum items often vary by geographic area, gender, age, and a whole host of other variables, you have the flexibility to interpret the items as needed and provide examples that will help others understand how the items apply to them.

DECEMBER 31

— *New Year's Eve* —

People usually pause to take a breath when talking. They may even wait a little before talking again. Sometimes it takes a while for people to formulate a thought or study your reaction to what they're saying. Such pauses do not mean that they are done talking. Wait at least three to five seconds to talk if you are unsure.

— *Something Fairly New and Very Important:* —
Context and Prediction

Understanding context and making predictions are essential to the human experience. Briefly, *context* refers to the setting or environment as well as individuals who are involved in that environment. And *prediction* is the ability to form a "best guess" based on observation and anticipate what is likely to happen. If someone has challenges with prediction and context, they may (a) cling to familiar activities; (b) be unwilling to willingly try new ventures or experience anxiety/behavior challenges when merely introduced to the possibility of participating in new activities; or (c) protest, refuse, or melt down when forced to engage in a new activity. To learn more about prediction and context, refer to Vermeulen (2012, 2023).

DECEMBER 30

When first getting to know somebody, consider doing a structured activity, such as going to a movie or playing mini-golf. These types of activities have a definite starting and ending time, and if you don't know what to say, it's OK because you don't have a lot of time to talk.

— *The Hidden Curriculum, Prediction and Context:* — *An Example*

In the morning, Ms. Brown, a fifth-grade teacher, presents one item from the calendar: "*Fair* means that everyone gets what everyone needs. It does not mean that everyone gets the same thing." She explains the item to her students using several examples. "*Fair* means that a person who cannot hear gets a hearing aid. *Fair* means that the shortest person in the class is probably on the first row in class pictures so they can be seen better. *Fair* means that some people who have trouble writing might do their assignments on the computer." She provides similar examples about *equal*. Then she asks students to explain what the item means. Ms. Brown also asks questions that include context and prediction: "What would happen if we were not *fair* to others?" (prediction) and, "Is there a time when it is OK to be equal and not fair?" (context). Ms. Brown also highlights a real-life example that helps students better understand *fair* and *equal*. She also challenges students to identify an incident of fairness to share the next day.

DECEMBER 29

If your mother makes you angry in the morning before you leave for school, it does not mean all other adults you run into throughout the day are trying to make your life miserable.

— *Suggestions for How to Use This Calendar* —

The hidden curriculum covers an infinite number of items, so teaching and mastering them can seem overwhelming to both teachers and learners. By approaching this task based on the saying, "A journey of a thousand miles begins with a single step," it seems less daunting.

If a teacher begins each day of school by overviewing one hidden curriculum rule and calling it to the attention of students when it happens during the day, a student can learn 180 items each year. Likewise, if parents present one item each evening as the child is going to bed or during breakfast, the child can be introduced to 365 hidden curriculum examples.

Schools could adopt the hidden curriculum calendar by having the principal or a student read an item during morning announcements and educational professionals and staff follow up with a discussion or by identifying real-life examples. In one middle school, the administrative assistant became known as the "hidden curriculum guy" because he always talked to students about items when they were introduced.

DECEMBER 28

Never throw food in the lunchroom,
even if other students do.

JANUARY 1

— New Year's Day —

Do not share hurtful information about someone unless it is helpful in some way. For example, it is generally not helpful to tell a person they are fat or unattractive. Share helpful information, such as telling someone quietly that they have their shirt buttoned wrong.

DECEMBER 27

If you have to blow your nose, do it discreetly rather than standing in the middle of a room and attracting attention.

JANUARY 2

Doing a favor for someone does not automatically mean they will do a favor for you. Do a favor for someone because you want to—not because you want the person to return the favor right away. That way, if they decide to do you a favor, you will be pleasantly surprised.

DECEMBER 26

It is not rude to be confident in your abilities. But telling other people they are not as good as you are at something is rude.

JANUARY 3

Do not ask to share someone's drink or offer to share your own. Unhealthy germs can be passed back and forth that way, so it is a good idea to keep from doing that.

DECEMBER 25

— Christmas Day —

No matter how good the food was, it is not OK to lick your plate. If you really liked what you ate, remember to order it again at that same restaurant or ask your parents to make it again if you ate it at home.

JANUARY 4

Count the number of items you have before you go into the express lane, and make sure you are not over the required number posted above the register.

DECEMBER 24

What works for your friend may not work for you. Just because your friend is able to goof around and not study until the last minute and still get good grades does not mean you will be able to do the same thing.

JANUARY 5

Try to be as polite as possible. Do not make negative comments.

DECEMBER 23

Appetizers are sometimes a part of the meal. Do not eat all of the food on the appetizer plate; it is supposed to be shared. Make sure everyone who wants some gets some.

JANUARY 6

> Fair means that everyone gets what everyone needs. It does not mean that everyone gets the same thing. Equal is when everyone gets the same thing. Fair is when everyone gets what they need.
>
> *(Lavoie, 1994)*

DECEMBER 22

If you don't know what you are supposed to be doing, one way to figure this out is to look around and see what other people are doing.

JANUARY 7

Always be on time. It is rude to make others wait for you.

DECEMBER 21

The "Do Not Drive on the Shoulder" road sign means that you (or your parents) cannot use the shoulder to drive on. It is there for safety. If you need to pull over or your car breaks down, you can drive on the shoulder to slow down or stop your car.

JANUARY 8

A purse, wallet, and backpack are personal and private items. Never open them if you do not have permission to do so.

DECEMBER 20

If you need to spit out something because it tastes bad, do it discreetly in your napkin and not onto your plate. And don't announce that you have just spit out your food.

JANUARY 9

Always wear your seat belt when riding in a car. Even if the driver does not wear a seat belt, be sure you do. Your safety is very important.

DECEMBER 19

It is important to know when you should be listening to your teacher. A good rule is to look toward your teacher when they are talking.

JANUARY 10

When you ask for help, it does not mean you are not smart; it means you are resourceful and want to solve a problem or get things done.

DECEMBER 18

If you receive a present you do not like, do not tell the person who gave it to you that you do not like it. They were thoughtful to give you a present. Say, "Thank you." Then make a positive comment about the present.

JANUARY 11

Always do what a police officer tells you to do. For example, if the officer asks you for identification, show it.

DECEMBER 17

If an actor on a stage asks a question, they usually do not want you to answer.

JANUARY 12

Call 911 in an emergency only.

DECEMBER 16

Try not to ask your parents if a friend can stay for supper in front of your friend. It is embarrassing to your friend and parents if they say no.

JANUARY 13

Brush your teeth well when you get up in the morning and at night before you go to bed.

DECEMBER 15

If you play on a team, don't blame others if you lose.

JANUARY 14

Be on time to class, parties, and meetings.

DECEMBER 14

If your parent is on the phone, consider very carefully whether it is necessary to interrupt them. Unless it is truly urgent, don't interrupt. Find something else to do until they are off the phone.

JANUARY 15

Body noises such as burping and passing gas are not to be shared with others. Say, "Pardon me," if you accidentally burp in front of others. If you pass gas, you may want to ignore it if others do not notice.

DECEMBER 13

If a parent tells you or your brother/sister to do something and you don't obey, it is the parent's responsibility to enforce discipline, not yours.

JANUARY 16

If you notice that another student forgot to zip a zipper, has a button unbuttoned, or has a piece of toilet paper stuck to their shoe, tell them quietly.

DECEMBER 12

Talk with your parents and develop a plan on where to meet them if you are separated at a store, park, or other area.

JANUARY 17

Change your undergarments and socks every day. They should be clean when you put them on.

DECEMBER 11

If you pass notes in class, keep in mind that it is probably against the teacher's rules. Also keep in mind that if a teacher catches you passing a note, they might read it out loud to the class. That might be embarrassing.

JANUARY 18

If someone makes a rude remark to you, it is best to try not to make a rude remark back.

DECEMBER 10

When hearing someone speak using incorrect grammar, do not correct them every time—especially in a critical way.

JANUARY 19

An invitation that includes an RSVP means that the people who are having the party need to know for sure if you are coming or not so that they can make plans.

DECEMBER 9

Toothpicks are usually available as you leave a restaurant. This is to encourage you to pick your teeth outside of the restaurant, if you have to. Also, your straw is not meant to be used as a toothpick.

JANUARY 20

— Martin Luther King, Jr. Day (USA) —

When eating, do not reach across other people to retrieve things, such as the breadbasket or salt and pepper shakers. Ask for them to be passed to you. This will keep your sleeves out of messes and will not spread germs.

DECEMBER 8

If you notice that someone has bad breath, it is not polite to say so. Instead, if you have a mint, you can take one out for yourself and ask the other person if they would like one.

JANUARY 21

Wash your hands after you sneeze and before you touch anything.

DECEMBER 7

It is not OK to give out private family information to a stranger on the phone or internet. There are people who pretend to be someone else on the phone or internet just so they can get your personal information. It is a good idea to know your parents' rule about what information is just for the family to discuss.

JANUARY 22

Cheering for your school team is great. However, there are some cheers crowds say that are rude and might get you into trouble, especially if you are the only one saying them.

DECEMBER 6

If you dance with someone, this does not automatically mean the person is your girlfriend or boyfriend. Likewise, if someone stands next to you in line for recess, that does not make that person your best friend.

JANUARY 23

Always wash your hands after you use the restroom.

DECEMBER 5

If you need to remove cords from electrical sockets, hold the plug and pull gently.

JANUARY 24

Breaking the law is never a good idea, no matter what your reason is. For example, if you need food or a pencil, it is better to ask for it instead of stealing.

DECEMBER 4

It is not polite to ask someone how much her clothes cost or volunteer how much you paid for something.

JANUARY 25

Friends say nice things to each other. They do not make negative comments unless they are playful, fun comments.

DECEMBER 3

If you lose something in a store, ask for the Lost and Found Department; it is usually in the customer service area.

JANUARY 26

Display your best behavior when in public. Things that are OK to do or talk about at home are not necessarily OK to do or talk about out in the community, such as private family matters.

DECEMBER 2

Never touch food on the buffet at a restaurant with your hands. There are usually serving utensils in the serving dishes. If you need to taste something before you decide to take a full serving of it, put a very tiny portion on your plate and taste it. Go back for more if you like it; if you don't, just leave it on a corner of your plate.

JANUARY 27

Cutting in line at school, at the store, movies, etc. is not fair to the people who have been waiting in line.

DECEMBER 1

When walking into a building or home, wipe your feet until you are certain there is nothing left on the bottom of your shoe to track inside. This is especially true in the winter or when the weather is bad outside.

JANUARY 28

Do not ask other people for money or food at lunchtime if you have money or food of your own.

NOVEMBER 30

Picking at scabs and sores in front of other people is gross. Sometimes it is unhealthy to do even if you are alone.

JANUARY 29

During silent reading, read in your mind, not out loud.

NOVEMBER 29

If someone asks you to lie, it is best to say, "I am sorry, but I can't do that."

JANUARY 30

At a fast-food restaurant, do not take more napkins, straws, ketchup, etc. than you need. If you take them and don't use them, they will be wasted. The restaurant owners still have to pay, but the things have to be thrown away, as nobody else wants to use them.

NOVEMBER 28

If you lose a game at recess, it's OK. Usually the reason you play a game is to learn new skills or enjoy time with other people. Winning is not the most important thing.

JANUARY 31

Do not go into other people's yards unless you are invited.

NOVEMBER 27

Don't walk up behind someone quietly without announcing yourself, especially if it is someone you don't know and it is dark outside. This can be very frightening. Make sure the person hears or sees you.

FEBRUARY 1

If someone plays with your toys or touches things at your house, it doesn't mean they will keep them. Sharing isn't the same as giving away.

NOVEMBER 26

If you let someone copy answers from your paper, you will most likely get an "F" even if you knew all the answers.

FEBRUARY 2

— Groundhog Day (US and Canada) —

During sporting events, it is normal to stand and cheer during the game. But do not stand the entire time unless everyone else is. If you do, you may obstruct the view of those around you.

NOVEMBER 25

In music class, if your neighbor sings off-key and it bothers you, go to your teacher after class and ask to be moved to a different seat. If you talk to your teacher during class, it might hurt the student's feelings.

FEBRUARY 3

Avoid talking to someone who is talking on the telephone. This makes it difficult for them to hear what the person on the other end of the phone is saying, as well as what you are saying.

NOVEMBER 24

If you must talk during a movie, speak in a whisper.

FEBRUARY 4

During group assignments in class, everybody in the group is responsible for doing the work. So participate but don't take over, even if you don't think the other students are doing it your way.

NOVEMBER 23

If you sleep over at a friend's house, you may not be on a bed, or you may not be sleeping in an area by yourself. If you worry about the arrangements, it's OK to ask ahead of time.

FEBRUARY 5

During the school day, you are only allowed to be in certain areas of the school. If you are not sure where you are allowed to be and when, ask a teacher or other adult.

NOVEMBER 22

Do not pull on your underwear to "fix" them unless you are in the bathroom or another private place.

FEBRUARY 6

— *Waitangi Day (New Zealand)* —

Sometimes students elbow each other when the teacher is not looking, just for fun. If you want to do this and do not want to get in trouble, stop before the teacher looks.

NOVEMBER 21

If you know what a person is getting for his birthday or a holiday, do not tell. If asked, just say that you cannot share that information because it is a secret. It is not a lie to keep this kind of information secret.

FEBRUARY 7

If you finish an assignment before the other students, work quietly at your desk until the teacher says to stop or turn the assignment in to the teacher. If you don't know which one to do, ask the teacher.

NOVEMBER 20

When someone says, "Hold on," they don't mean that you need to grabs something. They mean that you need to wait until they are ready for you to talk.

FEBRUARY 8

If someone gives you a gift, it is polite to write a thank-you note even if you say, "Thank you," when you open the gift.

NOVEMBER 19

It is wasteful to take more food than you can eat. Most of the time, there will still be food available if you want more.

FEBRUARY 9

At home or in restaurants, it is polite to wait until everyone is served to start eating. When everybody at your table starts eating, you may start.

NOVEMBER 18

If you think the teacher made a mistake in grading your paper, politely ask if you can talk with them about your assignment.

FEBRUARY 10

When you give Valentine cards to other students, it does not mean that you want them to be your boyfriend or girlfriend. It is sometimes a school tradition to give a Valentine to everyone.

NOVEMBER 17

Just because a person is very popular, it does not mean that they are a nice or good person to have as a friend.

FEBRUARY 11

It is not polite to blow your nose at the table. Excuse yourself and go to the bathroom to blow your nose. This will keep your dinner partners from getting grossed out.

NOVEMBER 16

Even if it is hard to control your body when you are upset, it is important to try to contain your body and words to protect yourself and your family. For example, if you hit one of your parents, others might misinterpret the situation and get involved, or even call the police.

FEBRUARY 12

During a fire drill, go with your class to the nearest exit to get outside. This is not the time to go to the bathroom or ask to go to the bathroom. Follow the teacher's directions.

NOVEMBER 15

If you are going on a plane trip, it is a good idea to use the restroom before you leave the airport. It could be a rather long time before you can get up and use the airplane restroom, and airplane restrooms are usually quite busy.

FEBRUARY 13

Daily showering and putting on deodorant will make you smell nicer and be easier to be around.

NOVEMBER 14

It is a good idea not to say every single thing you think. It might hurt people's feelings.

FEBRUARY 14

— Valentine's Day —

Being different is not bad or good. Different is just different. We are all different in some aspect of our lives. "Different" people have accomplished great things in life.

NOVEMBER 13

If you want to ask someone a favor, try to make sure that (1) they are in a good mood, and (2) they are not in a hurry.

FEBRUARY 15

If someone has something in his teeth or nose, quietly tell the person so that they can remove it privately.

NOVEMBER 12

— Veteran's Day (USA) —

When meeting someone new, such as an adult, it is polite to say, "I am pleased to meet you." When you meet someone your own age, you usually do not have to be this formal, but you should act interested in them.

FEBRUARY 16

At a restaurant, do not talk about other people sitting around you—do not comment on what they are eating, drinking, or smoking or what they look like.

NOVEMBER 11

In the lunchroom, begin eating right away so you can finish in time.

FEBRUARY 17

Do not pick on other students. Only weak people or people who do not have a good character pick on others.

NOVEMBER 10

It is a good general rule not to do what people do on television or in the movies—even if the show is called "reality."

FEBRUARY 18

Even if other students write in their textbooks or on their desks, don't do it. Use a piece of paper or Post-it instead so you won't get in trouble.

NOVEMBER 9

On a plane, don't hog the armrest or lean your chair back without first checking with your neighbors.

FEBRUARY 19

— President's Day (USA) —

Don't touch someone's hair even if it looks nice. You definitely should not smell it.

NOVEMBER 8

People like different types of music—opera, classical music, rock, rap. If someone likes a type of music that you don't, ask what they like about the music. You might learn something new and might even like the music in the future.

FEBRUARY 20

Be willing to try new activities and skills. Usually, the only way you know if you like something is to try it out.

NOVEMBER 7

It is best not to shake hands with someone if you have a cold, because you may be transmitting germs. You can say, "I would like to shake your hand, but I do not want to give you my cold."

FEBRUARY 21

Before starting to speak to somebody, it is a good idea to say the other person's name to get their attention.

NOVEMBER 6

When leaving a restaurant, never pick up money left on the table by others. It is polite to leave a tip at "sit-down" restaurants. The waiter or waitress earns their living by serving people well and receiving a good tip.

FEBRUARY 22

Understand the rules about shaking hands with others.

NOVEMBER 5

When you raise your hand to ask a question, the teacher may not answer until they finish their sentence.

FEBRUARY 23

Even if someone is smiling or laughing when you are tickling them, if they tell you to stop, stop immediately.

NOVEMBER 4

It is not OK to stare at people. It is especially rude to stare at people who have disabilities or who look or behave "differently" in any way.

FEBRUARY 24

When you are at a piano concert, school play, or similar event, try not to say, "Is this ever going to end?" or anything else that the performer may find offensive or negative. Even if you are not interested, it is rude to show that openly.

NOVEMBER 3

It is rude to talk on your phone while you should be doing something else, like listening to your teacher or a friend.

FEBRUARY 25

Blowing your nose into a handkerchief or tissue is acceptable and polite. Showing it to others is not.

NOVEMBER 2

Use one to two squirts of soap for washing your hands and one to two paper towels for drying your hands. Use only as much as you need.

FEBRUARY 26

Even if someone smells bad, it is probably not your job to tell them they smell bad. Telling someone the wrong way will hurt their feelings.

NOVEMBER 1

If someone borrows money from you and does not pay you back even if you have asked repeatedly, it is probably best not to loan them money again.

FEBRUARY 27

Do not hit others.

OCTOBER 31

— *Halloween* —

It is not a prank if someone gets hurt.
If you hurt someone, it is meanness.

FEBRUARY 28

Doing poorly on a test usually means that you need to learn a different way of studying. Talk with your parents and teachers so they can help you.

OCTOBER 30

It is not polite to interrupt others while they are talking, unless it is an emergency.

FEBRUARY 29

— Leap Day —

Do not throw anything off a bridge,
or it may hit people or cars below.

OCTOBER 29

Remember to use an inside voice in the doctor's waiting room and a whisper voice inside a library.

MARCH 1

Be aware that if you tell someone a secret, there is a chance the person will tell someone else—even if they are your friend.

OCTOBER 28

If you come to class without the necessary supplies (pencils, paper, etc.), ask someone if you can borrow them. Before you do this, know whom to ask. Some teachers are OK with letting students borrow supplies from classmates; others are not. If you ask another student, be sure it is someone who is friendly toward you.

MARCH 2

Find out when the teacher will allow you to work on homework or assignments from other classes.

OCTOBER 27

Walk inside the classroom and in most buildings, instead of running.

MARCH 3

Friendships take a lot of time to develop. Just because someone in your class was nice to you one time, it does not mean that he or she is your best friend.

OCTOBER 26

If your parent, teacher, or other adult says that they don't feel well or have a headache, they probably won't be as patient as they usually are. It isn't a good time to repeatedly ask questions, complain, or talk about your special interest. It might be better to steer clear of them until they feel better.

MARCH 4

Friends tell each other secrets and their likes and dislikes. Friendship is different from just meeting a person and talking to him or her.

OCTOBER 25

If you are throwing a ball to someone in the gym or at recess, say their name and wait until they look up and have their hands out before throwing it.

MARCH 5

Friends forgive each other
for mistakes they make.

OCTOBER 24

On the playground, there is not enough equipment for all the kids to have their own. Students need to share and take turns using the equipment.

MARCH 6

You should not have to pay someone to be your friend.

OCTOBER 23

It is important to learn how to calculate and receive change at a store. Sometimes mistakes are made. Most are accidents.

MARCH 7

Control your anger. In some places, displaying strong anger in public can get you kicked out. It might even get you arrested.

OCTOBER 22

When playing tag, touch softly
as if you are petting a dog.

MARCH 8

Do not touch other people without permission.

OCTOBER 21

Limit the number of questions you ask in class. If you continue to ask questions, it may bother the other students and the teacher. If you have a lot of questions, ask the teacher privately before or after class.

MARCH 9

Don't put your feet on the back of the seat in front of you if someone is sitting there.

OCTOBER 20

Others may not always agree with you, or you may not agree with others when talking about things; that's OK. Everyone is entitled to his or her own opinion.

MARCH 10

Never let people (friends, strangers, or adults) store backpacks or other bags in your locker without asking to see what is inside. If someone puts something illegal in your locker, you could get into trouble even if you didn't have anything to do with it.

OCTOBER 19

It is usually OK to tell the waiter in a polite way that you are not happy with your food. Tell the waiter exactly what is wrong with your food, but don't be rude or blame the waiter.

MARCH 11

Even if you do not like someone, it is OK to think that to yourself. Don't say, "I don't like you," directly to the person.

OCTOBER 18

If someone calls to you, acknowledge that you heard. For example, if your mom calls you for dinner, say something like, "OK, I'll be right there." If you don't respond, people think you are ignoring them and may get mad or hurt.

MARCH 12

When someone says, "Make yourself at home," it generally doesn't mean that you should act at that person's house the way you do at your house.

OCTOBER 17

Use a "nice" voice when talking to others during conversation. If your voice sounds angry, even if your words are kind, they may be misunderstood.

MARCH 13

Hold the door open for someone older than you or when someone is close behind you.

OCTOBER 16

It is OK to cover your ears to drown out the sound of the fire alarm when you are exiting the building.

MARCH 14

You may get bumped in a crowded hallway. It is usually an accident, so try not to get too upset.

OCTOBER 15

Take care of other people's property as well as or better than you take care of your own.

MARCH 15

It is usually important to go to the bathroom before you leave the house. Even though you are only going on a short trip, such as to the grocery store, you never know when things can change.

OCTOBER 14

Use a pleasant voice when talking to teachers, because they will respond to you in a more positive way.

MARCH 16

Do not pick on others. Only weak people or people who do not have a good character pick on others.

OCTOBER 13

When playing a game with teams, usually everyone likes to have a turn. Encourage your teammates to do well and stay on the same team throughout the game.

MARCH 17

— *St. Patrick's Day* —

You don't have to give other people your stuff just because they ask for it. It is OK to keep your own things.

OCTOBER 12

When playing a game, you will not always get to follow the rules you have at home. You must follow the rules the group chooses or choose not to play the game.

MARCH 18

If a classmate of the opposite sex is nice to you, this does not mean they want to be your boyfriend/girlfriend. Going around and telling your classmates and friends will make the person upset and probably ruin your chances in the future.

OCTOBER 11

If you notice that someone has passed gas, the correct thing to do is to pretend that you did not notice.

MARCH 19

You do not have to spend every penny you have. Saving your money for something big gives you time to decide if you really want it and if it is worth the price.

OCTOBER 10

It is important to use people's names when talking to them.

MARCH 20

You do not have to comment every time someone tells you a story about themselves. Most people would see you as a "know-it-all" and would eventually stop talking to you.

OCTOBER 9

It is inappropriate to comment on the quality of other students' work, unless the entire class is discussing how they can improve their work.

MARCH 21

Writing something in your own handwriting is not the same as making something up. If you copy someone else's words but hand them in as your own, that is plagiarism and can get you into serious trouble.

OCTOBER 8

Saying, "Shut up," to somebody is not appropriate in most instances. It is generally better to ask someone to please stop talking.

MARCH 22

If someone intrudes on your space, ask him politely to move over without touching him.

OCTOBER 7

If you need to cough or sneeze, cover your mouth and move your head a little away from the table or other people. Then use a tissue. When finished, wrap the tissue, put it in your pocket, and say, "Excuse me." Later, you can throw the tissue away.

MARCH 23

Hugging is usually OK if the other person is a parent, family member, or friend. But don't suddenly hug them in public.

OCTOBER 6

It is not appropriate to use other people's locker items or things in someone's desk or purse without asking and receiving permission first.

MARCH 24

Even though you have completed your assignment according to the directions, you will probably get more points for making your work as neat as possible. Write clearly, and avoid crumpling the paper or erasing until the paper tears.

OCTOBER 5

It is not polite to spit in public, especially on the sidewalk or in a public trashcan. If you have gum in your mouth and you need to get rid of it, put it into a tissue and throw it away.

MARCH 25

If someone bullies you to get something from you, quietly tell an adult you trust.

OCTOBER 4

If you borrow something, return it in the same condition you received it or replace it.

MARCH 26

Who you are with often determines what to talk about. For example, you can talk about a new song with a friend. You probably would not do that with an adult.

OCTOBER 3

It is not OK to give medicine
to your friends at school,
even if it's Tylenol or Advil.

MARCH 27

While working in class, keep your eyes on your own paper.

OCTOBER 2

It is OK to be loud on the playground or talk in a louder voice (not yelling) in the halls during passing period. When it is time to go back inside or it is time for class, you must be quiet.

MARCH 28

Even if you are wearing headphones, keep the volume of your device down so that people around you cannot hear your music.

OCTOBER 1

It's OK to make a mistake
on your paper and correct it.

MARCH 29

If other students are fighting or bullying others, tell the teacher. If they are goofing around, do not tell the teacher. You can usually tell if they are just goofing around if nobody is upset or getting hurt. If you cannot tell the difference, quietly ask a friend or teacher.

SEPTEMBER 30

Just because someone shares their lunch with you one day does not automatically mean that they will share their lunch with you again.

MARCH 30

Get a clean plate for each trip you make to the buffet at a restaurant. This is not only the law; it is also a nice thing to do. No one wants to see what you already ate, and you do not want to eat something that fell off someone else's plate.

SEPTEMBER 29

It is OK to try food if free samples are given out at the grocery store. Usually you should try only one of each sample.

MARCH 31

Words and phrases that are idioms and metaphors do not always mean exactly what they say. For example, if someone says, "See you later, alligator," he is not calling you a reptile. If someone uses a phrase that does not make sense, ask that person what it means.

SEPTEMBER 28

If you do not want to do an assignment, you can think that in your head. You still have to do it. If you say something out loud, you may get in trouble.

APRIL 1

When a friend tells you a secret and that secret involves something that will hurt someone or something illegal, your friend will expect you to keep that secret.

SEPTEMBER 27

When shaking hands with an adult, remember to look toward the person and grip their hand firmly, but not so firmly that it hurts.

APRIL 2

When someone says, "Make yourself at home," it generally means that you should act at that person's house the way you do at your house.

SEPTEMBER 26

When you are waiting for an elevator and the doors open, allow the people who are getting off to do so before you enter the elevator.

APRIL 3

When your parents are mad at you, it is not a good time to point out the various reasons why something is their fault and not yours, question their intelligence, or ask them for something. To help your parents calm down more quickly, act sorry, even if you are not sure you are.

SEPTEMBER 25

People often judge you within the first few minutes of meeting you. Try to remember this and make a good impression by being polite and attentive to others.

APRIL 4

Flight attendants have very important jobs to do. While they are almost always friendly, this does not mean they have time to be your friend. If you need to ask them a question and it is not an emergency, wait until they come to offer you a drink or a blanket.

SEPTEMBER 24

Teachers give students "transition statements" to let them know that a new activity or other change will happen. Learn what your teacher uses so you can be ready to go to the next subject or activity. Some teachers may tell you that you will be leaving in five minutes. That usually does not mean exactly five minutes; it may mean two minutes or ten minutes. It is to let you know that you will be leaving soon.

APRIL 5

If you get a present that you already have, don't say, "Oh, I've already got five of these. Where can I take it back?" Instead, say something like, "This is a great gift." It is a great gift—it was so good that you already have one. You can exchange it later.

SEPTEMBER 23

When at a small formal ceremony where someone is being recognized, do not yell and scream unless everyone else does. Wait to see what the audience does and follow along.

APRIL 6

Do not hit others.

SEPTEMBER 22

Be sure that you flush the toilet after you use it. Other people do not want to walk in and look at what you left in the toilet.

APRIL 7

When your parents are lecturing you, it is not a good time to bring up something that has nothing to do with the conversation. Parents take this as a sign that you are not listening. This makes parents annoyed, and they might give you an even longer lecture.

SEPTEMBER 21

If a teacher says he doesn't like to hear certain words, it means you will get into trouble if you say those words in class. So don't do it.

APRIL 8

When you want to help another student with a worksheet, do not grab the paper and do it yourself. Let the student keep their own paper and ask if they would like you to explain the answer. If the student says no, stop right there.

SEPTEMBER 20

Teachers use nonverbal communication to send messages to students. Sometimes teachers *look at* students, *stand close* to them, or *raise* or *lower their* voices to get their message across. If you do not know what the teacher is trying to communicate, ask politely.

APRIL 9

When eating at a friend's home, wait until the head of the house (usually a parent) says the food is ready. Do not go to the kitchen to see what is for dinner and ask when the food will be ready.

SEPTEMBER 19

When it is time to clean up after class, follow your teacher's rules for clean-up. It usually does not have to be perfectly clean. The janitor will come in after school to vacuum and do the final clean-up.

APRIL 10

Try not to read over someone's shoulder when they are texting or emailing. It is private information that they might not want you to see.

SEPTEMBER 18

When someone is speaking to you, it makes the person feel like you are really listening if you look at them, nod once in a while, and say things like, "Yeah," or, "OK." If you are listening to an adult, try to say, "Yes," instead of, "Yeah."

APRIL 11

Surprise your parents by looking around to see what needs to be done and then doing it without being asked first. You will feel good about yourself, and you might get to laugh at the shocked expression on your parents' faces. They will be so happy.

SEPTEMBER 17

Take care of your personal appearance (runny nose, wet clothes, etc.). Think about keeping your hair brushed or combed, carry a packet of tissues with you if your nose is runny, or keep a change of clothes handy (either in your locker, the nurse's office, or at home where you can easily find them) in case you fall into a mud puddle or sit in something sticky.

APRIL 12

If you have a guest speaker in class, do not interrupt the speech. Ask questions at the end. There is usually set time aside for questions afterward.

SEPTEMBER 16

Talk to your teachers and other adults in a different way than you talk to your friends.

APRIL 13

When you want to play or do things with someone, do not pressure them if they tell you no.

SEPTEMBER 15

When asked, "How is your meal?" be polite even if you do not like the food. It is kind to say, "Thank you for cooking such a nice meal."

APRIL 14

Most people cannot smell their own breath. Use mints or gum to make sure your breath does not make people stand far away from you because they don't like your breath.

SEPTEMBER 14

On the tests where teachers cannot help you with answers, you can usually ask questions if they are not on the test, such as, "Can I borrow a pencil?" or, "May I go to the restroom?"

APRIL 15

In class, students usually raise their hands to get the teacher's attention. Know the teacher's rules about getting help.

SEPTEMBER 13

When you are trying on shoes in a store, wear socks, or if you are not, ask a store employee for special throw-away socks or bring your own socks.

APRIL 16

Do not pick on others. Only weak people or people who do not have a good character pick on others.

SEPTEMBER 12

Take responsibility for your actions.

APRIL 17

When the teacher is giving a lesson, it is time to pay attention and listen. You can talk about topics that you are interested in at another time.

SEPTEMBER 11

When meeting someone new, such as an adult, it is polite to say, "I am pleased to meet you." When you meet someone your own age, you usually do not have to be this formal, but you should act interested in them.

APRIL 18

If you have made plans with someone and you get an opportunity to do something else, it is not appropriate to cancel the plans you made first, even if the second plans are more fun.

SEPTEMBER 10

If your teacher gives you a warning to stop a certain behavior and you continue the behavior, you will probably get in trouble. If you stop the behavior immediately after the warning, you will probably not get into trouble.

APRIL 19

Talk with your parents and develop a plan on where to meet them if you are separated at a store, park, or other area.

SEPTEMBER 9

When someone else is getting in trouble, it is not a good time to ask questions or show the teacher something.

APRIL 20

Picking up broken glass with your fingers is almost never a good idea.

SEPTEMBER 8

When you don't know the answer to a question, it is often best to admit that you don't know the answer and ask for help.

APRIL 21

Stay away from people who get you into trouble.

SEPTEMBER 7

Learn the rules of the games played at recess or PE by asking another student, your parents, or the teacher.

APRIL 22

— Earth Day —

It is not OK to throw trash out of the car window. It is illegal and is bad for the environment.

SEPTEMBER 6

If you receive the wrong change in a restaurant or store, calmly tell the waiter or clerk that you did not receive the correct amount of money. Tell them what type of money you gave them and how much change you were expecting. In most cases, the short-changing is an accident.

APRIL 23

For your own comfort, wear clothes that are appropriate for the weather. In many parts of the country, shorts and sandals would not be enough protection in the winter, and wool pants or shirts would be too hot in the summer.

SEPTEMBER 5

When you are finished using the toilet, fix your clothing before coming out of the stall. (Pull up and zip your pants, tuck your shirt back in, make sure your skirt is not stuck in the waistband of your underwear, etc.)

APRIL 24

Learn when it is OK to tattle. If someone is getting hurt or is getting their feelings hurt, it is usually right to tell. It is also OK to tell if someone is going to do something illegal. If you do not know whether to tattle, quietly ask an adult, "Would you like to know if one person is ... ?"

SEPTEMBER 4

When you are at school, walking down the hall to go to your class, if an adult calls to you, stop. Even if you are worried about being late to class, you need to stop and listen to what they have to say.

APRIL 25

— ANZAC Day
(Australia and New Zealand) —

If you have asked your parents for something several times in a short period of time and the answer is no, it is a pretty safe bet that the answer is still no a couple of minutes later. Don't keep asking. All you will accomplish is to make them angry.

SEPTEMBER 3

Fair means that everyone gets what everyone needs. It does not mean that everyone gets the same thing. *Equal* is when everyone gets the same thing. *Fair* is when everyone gets what they need.

APRIL 26

If other students are teasing you, do not get mad and hit them. Tell them politely to stop. If they don't stop, privately ask an adult for help. Most adults know how to stop the teasing without it being traced back to you.

SEPTEMBER 2

When you are assigned to a group, stay with that group until the teacher changes the assignment.

APRIL 27

When you walk up to someone's house, don't look into the windows or doors. That is rude and, sometimes, even dangerous.

SEPTEMBER 1

Replace the cap on any pen or marker that you have used so it doesn't dry out or smear on things.

APRIL 28

When you try to find a seat to sit in, make sure that someone else isn't planning to sit there. If you are not sure, ask people around you if the seat is available.

AUGUST 31

If you wish to tell a joke or story more than once, find another person to tell it to.

APRIL 29

Elbowing other people in line
is wrong. Make sure you know
why you are elbowing someone,
and don't poke too hard.

AUGUST 30

Work with your family to develop a rule about giving money to somebody in the street who is asking for money. For example, parents may have rules such as, "Only give money to someone when you are with an adult."

APRIL 30

When standing in a line, make sure there is enough space for one or two people between you and the person in front of you unless it is a very tight situation.

AUGUST 29

Seek out an adult if you are hurt or cannot handle a certain situation. For example, if you think someone is being mean to you, find an adult to tell.

MAY 1

Sometimes people bend the truth a little if it means sparing someone's feelings. For instance, if asked, do not tell your mom she looks fat even if you think she does. This is called a "white lie."

AUGUST 28

When you are sitting in the doctor's waiting room, do not ask other patients why they are there or tell them in detail why you are. Only tell the receptionist, nurse, and doctor why you are there when they ask.

MAY 2

It is OK to be mad at your friend sometimes. Tell your friend politely that what he did made you mad and try to work out your differences. Sometimes it is OK to "agree to disagree."

AUGUST 27

If someone, such as your parent or teacher, tells you to do something and you don't, they will probably be upset when they find out you did not do it.

MAY 3

If someone asks you a personal question like how much money your parents make or how much you weigh, it is OK to say that you are uncomfortable answering.

AUGUST 26

Some words have double meanings, like the word key. Sometimes the word means a metal object; at other times it means a plastic credit card–like pass often used to open doors. When someone says to use a key in a hotel room or other place, keep this in mind.

MAY 4

When you stay at a friend's house, follow their family's routine, not your typical home routine.

AUGUST 25

When speaking to someone,
look toward their face or eyes.
This will help the person realize
you are speaking to them.

MAY 5

— *Cinco de Mayo* —

There are certain questions you do not ask others if you have just met them. These include their weight, age, income, religion, etc.

AUGUST 24

Some pranks are against the law. If you want to do a prank, find out the consequences. If you get caught doing a prank, you may get a fine or even be sent to jail.

MAY 6

Never call your teacher or another adult a bad name. It is also impolite to call children and adolescents bad names.

AUGUST 23

If you wear the same distinct clothing every day, people will probably notice and make comments. For example, if you wear camouflage pants every day, even if it is a different pair every day, people will think you are not changing your clothes. Similarly, if you wear the same Nike T-shirt every day, it will seem like you do not change your clothes.

MAY 7

If your team loses,
congratulate the other team.

AUGUST 22

Make sure you pay for the items you picked up before leaving the store.

MAY 8

If your team wins, be
kind to the losing team.

AUGUST 21

Take turns in conversation.
Wait for the other person to
finish talking and then answer.

MAY 9

If you do something funny, it is usually only funny once. If you do it repeatedly, it makes you look silly (not in a good way).

AUGUST 20

When people ask how you are doing, they generally just want a short statement, such as, "I'm great! How are you?" Therefore, when answering, don't go into a long explanation about what's going on in your life.

MAY 10

If someone gets a puzzle game or computer game that you already have, let them figure out the solution on their own unless they ask for your help. If they want help, you might want to ask whether they want the solution or just a clue.

AUGUST 19

Repeating a joke after someone else has said it to the class will probably make others laugh at you or make the teacher look at you as a troublemaker.

MAY 11

Wear underwear when trying on swimsuits before you buy them.

AUGUST 18

If you respond with no enthusiasm to someone who is talking enthusiastically with you, they will probably stop talking with you. Try to be excited about the things your friends are excited about, even if for a little while—unless it is something that is harmful, illegal, etc.

MAY 12

Most families have rules that are different from those at your house. When you are visiting, respect others' way of doing things.

AUGUST 17

Talk with your parents about how much money you should ever loan someone and to whom you should loan money, if at all.

MAY 13

If you disagree with what a teacher is saying, politely say what you think and wait for an answer. If you still disagree, it is usually best to let it go.

AUGUST 16

On some tests, teachers are not allowed to help you answer questions on the test. They are not being mean. That is just the rule.

MAY 14

Do not slurp the last bit of your soda or milkshake loudly through the straw, even if you are trying to get the very last sip. The noise is rude.

AUGUST 15

Unless you have specific permission to do so, it is not polite to call someone after 9:00 at night. Some people may have an earlier "do not call" time. In addition, it is a good idea not to call someone in the morning before 9:00 unless they are expecting your call.

MAY 15

If you break something at someone else's home, tell an adult. It is not OK to just throw away the broken item or hide it.

AUGUST 14

Teachers do not know all the answers. It is OK if they need to look something up or ask someone else.

MAY 16

If you are not interested in what somebody is talking about, try to act interested and talk about what the person is interested in for a short time. Then you can change the subject to something that interests you.

AUGUST 13

When the principal or another person in authority says to you, "Come to the office," or "Come here," this is not a request. It is an order.

MAY 17

If a teacher tells another to do something and they don't obey, it is the teacher's responsibility to enforce discipline, not yours.

AUGUST 12

When you are asking your parents for something, remember that there is often a difference between what you *want* and what you *need*. You might need a new pair of shoes for school, but you might want them to be name-brand shoes. While your parents might agree that you need shoes, they may not agree on a certain brand.

MAY 18

Do not clip your nails, floss your teeth, put on deodorant, or do other grooming activities in public.

AUGUST 11

When walking with someone, walk alongside the person, not way ahead or behind, unless there is not enough room on the sidewalk or in the hallway.

MAY 19

If someone is making fun of another student, do not laugh or even listen. It is hurtful to the person who is being made fun of. You may want to think about what you can do to be helpful.

AUGUST 10

When you are in a public place and you are having a meltdown and your parents are trying to help you calm down or leave, it is dangerous to yell, "Help!" or, "Let go of me!" because other people could misinterpret the situation. They might think your parents are hurting you or that they are not your parents but someone trying to kidnap you and might call the police.

MAY 20

If someone never asks you to play, it is not a good idea to ask them to play every day.

AUGUST 9

If you have a short question, it is OK to bypass the line in a department store when other people are making purchases. Wait by the cash register and quickly ask your question when the cashier is ringing up the customer or waiting for the customer to pay.

MAY 21

When eating in a group, don't ask to try someone else's food if you are not willing to have them try yours.

AUGUST 8

When the teacher says, "Do your best," it means that you need to try your hardest. It does not mean that you will get 100 percent on the assignment.

MAY 22

Adults do not like it when kids point out the things they are doing wrong (even if they arc). It is not your responsibility to teach grownups how to do things. It's usually better just to keep quiet. The exception is an emergency.

AUGUST 7

When two people are standing close and speaking very softly, they are having a private conversation. Generally, do not join such a conversation without asking first. If the people are two of your really good friends, you can probably join the conversation. If you are unsure, it is best to ask.

MAY 23

It is not OK to tell jokes at funerals.

AUGUST 6

When watching a movie you have already seen, it is not polite to tell others what will happen next or how the movie ends.

MAY 24

If there is a line for the restroom, just do your necessary bathroom business so people don't have to wait too long. If there is no line for the bathroom, you can quickly do additional personal grooming in the bathroom (like brushing or flossing your teeth, combing your hair, cleaning your nails).

AUGUST 5

When you go to someone's house, don't kick off your shoes, lie on the couch, or help yourself to food from the refrigerator unless the adults have given you permission to do so.

MAY 25

If your parents say, "Just a minute," say, "OK." Don't say, "No, I can't wait," while stomping your foot. The exception is if you need to go to the bathroom really badly or you are about to throw up and need their help.

AUGUST 4

Every teacher usually has different rules. It is important to know the rules for each teacher. It will do no good to argue that everyone should have the same rules.

MAY 26

Never get into a car with somebody you don't know, even if the person wants to show you a puppy or give you candy. You must have direct permission from your parents to ride in someone's car.

AUGUST 3

When walking up and down staircases,
stay on the right side so others can pass.

MAY 27

If the teacher crosses her arms and clears her throat, she usually either wants the class to be quiet or to look up and get ready to listen.

AUGUST 2

Know which doors you need to knock on before entering a room.

MAY 28

If someone picks on you or calls you mean namcs, tell a trusted adult, such as a teacher. These students are not your friends.

AUGUST 1

If you get in trouble once, it does not mean that your entire day is ruined.

MAY 29

If someone speaks to you while you are wearing headphones, remove your headphones to give the person your full attention. You will also be able to hear better.

JULY 31

Waiting is a life skill. No matter where you are or what you do, you will have to wait sometimes. Learn how to wait by bringing a book to read, listening to music or a podcast, or playing a game quietly.

MAY 30

If you dance with someone, this does not automatically mean the person is your girlfriend or your boyfriend. Likewise, if someone stands next to you in line for recess, that does not make that person your best friend.

JULY 30

If you argue with a friend over every little thing, you will probably not be friends for long. Decide what things are just not worth fighting about, like which dog breed is best or which flavor of ice cream the world likes better.

MAY 31

It is important to face a speaker or position yourself in the direction of the speaker. That way the person knows you are paying attention.

JULY 29

If you forget the name of somebody you just met, tell them politely, "I'm sorry, I forgot your name." The person will usually tell you their name.

JUNE 1

Never eat or drink anything you take out of the garbage can, even if it looks fine.

JULY 28

If you are uncomfortable talking to people, it is OK to practice at home what you might say to someone at school, church or a club meeting. There are some topics, called "ice breakers" (weather, sports, or TV), that just about everyone can use to begin a conversation. Ask adults or siblings for ideas.

JUNE 2

When you meet your friend's parents for the first time, do not tell them about problems you are having or secret things you did with your friend.

JULY 27

There aren't many times when it's OK to point. It is never OK to point with your middle finger.

JUNE 3

When using public transportation, it is not OK to clip your nails, floss your teeth, or do other grooming activities except in the restroom.

JULY 26

Keep personal information about your family to yourself during school or in the community.

JUNE 4

When other seats are available at the movies, leave a space between yourself and a stranger.

JULY 25

Unless specifically told to sing along,
do not sing along with soloists,
ensembles, or choirs in a performance.

JUNE 5

If a friend has recently been to a funeral, they probably do not want to talk about what the dead person looked like. Don't ask for details unless the other person offers.

JULY 24

When you are at someone's home for a meal, eat what you are served if there are no choices. If you do not like what is being served, say, "Just a little bit, please. I'm not very hungry," instead of, "I don't want any. I don't like it."

JUNE 6

If a group of your friends is talking badly about another one of your friends, you can politely suggest that they talk to that friend rather than about her. Also remember that if they are talking about someone else to you, they are probably talking about you to someone else. Try not to be part of that kind of talk.

JULY 23

When saying the Pledge of Allegiance or singing/hearing the "Star-Spangled Banner," refrain from talking or laughing.

JUNE 7

If you are borrowing something from another student, do not put it in your mouth (like a pen).

JULY 22

When someone asks, "How do you like my new _____," they really want you to tell them you like it. Even if you don't like it, try to find something positive to say about it. If you can't think of something to say, sometimes you can just say, "Wow!" with enthusiasm.

JUNE 8

It is not OK to urinate in swimming pools or hot tubs.

JULY 21

When you are walking your dog, carry a pooper scooper or plastic bag to use to pick up after your dog.

JUNE 9

When looking for your item in the Lost and Found Department, it is not OK to take something that is not yours even if you really like it.

JULY 20

Know what the rule is for leaving the dinner table. In some families, a child may not leave the table until the head of the house (usually a parent) gets up. In other families, a child may ask to be excused when she is finished eating. It is OK to ask the adult what the rule is.

JUNE 10

Sometimes arguing with your parents, even if you know you are in the right, gets you into more trouble than saying nothing. "Winning" an argument is not always important.

JULY 19

Know which doors you should knock on. It is often best for someone to know that you are coming over before you visit.

JUNE 11

If a party or other event states that it ends at a certain time, make sure you are ready to leave by that time.

JULY 18

When people are crying or angry, try not to laugh, as it will make them feel worse.

JUNE 12

If your parents are carrying groceries into the house, it is nice to offer to help or at least open the door for them. People feel frustrated when they need help and others don't notice.

JULY 17

When you meet someone who is walking a dog, ask if it is OK before petting the dog, because the dog may not be friendly.

JUNE 13

If you use the last of the toilet paper, get out another roll for the next person who uses the restroom. If you arc at someone else's home, politely tell the host that the toilet paper needs to be replaced. Try to do this before someone else needs to use the restroom.

JULY 16

Sandwiches, wraps, chips and dip, and other "finger foods" are finger friendly, but most other foods require utensils. If the food is messy, it probably needs to be eaten using a knife and fork.

JUNE 14

— Flag Day (USA) —

If you are having trouble with an assignment, it is appropriate to ask nicely for help.

JULY 15

If you see a bee or other stinging insect, don't scream or throw a fit, because then it might sting you. Hold still until it flies away, or slowly and quietly leave. If it lands on your body, don't slap at it. Brush it off swiftly.

JUNE 15

If you wake up your parents early in the morning to ask them for something, they will probably tell you no. Wait for a better time even if you think it's important. This does not apply in emergencies, such as if there is a fire.

JULY 14

— Bastille Day (France) —

It is usually not OK to call adults by their first names without their permission. If you don't know whether to call them by their first or last name, just ask them.

JUNE 16

When you invite someone to your house, it is a good idea to alternate playing/doing what you both want to do. For examplc, you can both do something that your guest wants to do first, such as playing a game. Then you can both do what you want to do, such as watching a video.

JULY 13

When someone says, "Just a minute," they don't mean sixty seconds. They mean "sometime soon."

JUNE 17

Some people just aren't nice.
However, treat people as nicely
as you wish for them to treat you.

JULY 12

If someone does not answer when you knock on the door or ring the doorbell, come back later. Do not let yourself in even if the door is not locked.

JUNE 18

If you are carrying money with you, do not show it to other people or talk about how much money you have, especially to strangers.

JULY 11

When making conversation, avoid telling others constantly how good you are at something. Even if you are really good at sports statistics, for example, do not constantly brag about how good you are. This usually makes other kids avoid being around you.

JUNE 19

— *Juneteenth (USA)* —

If you have something that you really value at your home and do not want to share it with anyone, put it away *before* a person comes to visit.

JULY 10

When you get in or out of a car, keep your feet off the seat so it doesn't get dirty and leave a mess for someone else to sit in.

JUNE 20

If you are having a conversation with someone, don't stand in the middle of the hallway, sidewalk, or aisle. Move to the side.

JULY 9

When you are talking to a friend and you need to ask your parent something, set the phone down, hold it away from your mouth, or put it on mute if you are yelling for your parent. Otherwise, you will be yelling in the caller's ear.

JUNE 21

If a teacher tells another student to stop talking, it is a good idea for you to stop talking as well, since the teacher has already made it known that talking is not acceptable at that moment.

JULY 8

People act differently in different situations. Sometimes people will not treat you the same when they are around certain people.

JUNE 22

If your parent's bedroom door is closed, don't bother them unless it is an emergency. An emergency is something that cannot wait.

JULY 7

If you ask someone to do something with you and they say no, don't keep asking.

JUNE 23

If you are on a bus, subway, or park bench, don't take up more than one seat by spreading out your stuff.

JULY 6

Always wear a life jacket when riding in a boat. It is the law that boats have enough life jackets for everyone on the boat.

JUNE 24

If you are riding in someone's car and the car is messy, you don't need to say so. It is polite to say, "Thank you for the ride."

JULY 5

If someone gets hurt at a ballgame, it is a sign of support when people clap. They are not doing it because they think it's great.

JUNE 25

If you cannot think of something nice to say about someone, it is usually best to say nothing at all.

JULY 4

— Independence Day (USA) —

When you are in a nice restaurant, do not tell stories that contain the word "blood" or that might be considered gross, scary, or disgusting. That may cause people to lose their appetites.

JUNE 26

When you are at a store, it is not OK to make comments to people about what they are buying or what someone else in the store is buying.

JULY 3

Use a leash for your dog
when taking him for a walk.

JUNE 27

When you get on an elevator, always stand facing the doors; do not face the back or sides of the elevator. That way you will be able to watch the numbers for your floor, and you will be ready to exit the elevator when the elevator stops on your floor.

JULY 2

People like it when you smile at them while you are greeting them. It means that you are happy to see them. Even if you are not happy to see them, it is polite to smile to make them feel good.

JUNE 28

If one of your classmates tells you to do something you think might get you in trouble, stop and think before acting. Friends do not ask their friends to do things that will get them in trouble.

JULY 1

Some people like you to take your shoes off before you enter their house. If this is their rule, just follow it. There is no need to ask them why.

JUNE 29

When someone standing in the street asks you for money, you do not have to give him money. You do not have to tell him how much money you have. The person may look like he needs money, but you still do not have to give any.

JUNE 30

Never joke about robbing the bank when you are in one. The employees might think you are serious and call the police.

*— Halfway Point —
time to turn your
calendar around!*